Gold

Jaime Schwartz

Contents

Golden Treasures

What do you think of when you hear the word **gold**? Do you think of being rich? Do you think of gold medals or piles of gold bars? Maybe you see a treasure chest overflowing with beautiful gold jewelry and coins.

Throughout history, gold has been a symbol of wealth and power. People have risked their lives searching for gold. Wars have been fought over gold. **Empires** have been created and destroyed because of gold.

The Midas Touch

Long ago, the Greeks made up this story about the power of gold. It is the story of King Midas.

King Midas was very rich. He had a lot of gold. But he wanted more. He asked the gods to grant him a wish.

Midas wished that anything he touched would turn to gold. The gods granted his wish. Everything Midas touched turned to gold.

Midas touched his chair and it became a gold throne. His drinking cup became a gold goblet. Midas kept touching things so that they would turn to gold. Soon, Midas had more gold than anyone.

Midas grew hungry. He touched his food and it turned to gold. He could not eat. He was thirsty, too. But when he touched the water in his cup it turned to gold.

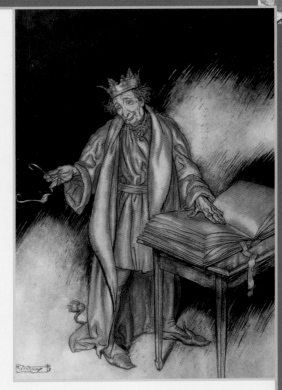

Then his daughter came to him. The only thing that Midas loved more than gold was his daughter. He hugged her. His daughter became a golden statue.

Midas cried. He begged the gods to bring his daughter back to life. They granted his wish. Midas never wanted gold again.

Today, people who are successful are said to have the "Midas touch."

A Valuable Resource

Gold is a metal. It is bright and shiny. More than any other metal, gold is valued for its beauty.

Gold is also a useful metal. It is one of the heaviest metals. It is twice as heavy as lead. But gold is soft, too. It is easy to work with. Gold can be hammered into very thin wire or shaped into a beautiful piece of jewelry.

▼ **This belt was made from gold.**

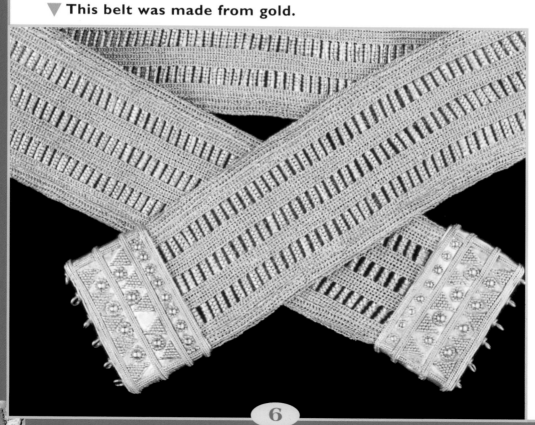

Gold is almost impossible to destroy or harm. Gold does not lose its shine the way silver does. Gold does not rust or flake like iron. Nothing seems to harm gold. Old gold treasure found beneath the sea can look the same as it did hundreds of years before it was buried. Time and salt water don't harm buried gold.

Gold is a **nonrenewable resource.** That means that there is a limited amount of gold in the ground. Once gold is taken from Earth, it cannot be replaced.

The **demand** for gold is high. But not enough gold is mined to **supply** all the people who want it. This keeps the price of gold high.

▼ **Lumps of gold are called nuggets. Gold nuggets are rare.**

Where Gold Is Found

Gold is found in rocks, in soil, and at the bottom of streams and rivers. Most of the gold produced today comes from rock. The rock containing gold, or **ore**, may be near the surface or buried deep in the ground.

▼ **The gold within this piece of ore sparkles.**

Deposits of gold are found around the world. About half of the world's gold is found in South Africa. The biggest gold field is located there. Large deposits of gold are also found in the United States and Australia. Look at the map. In what other countries is gold found?

Leading Gold Producing Nations

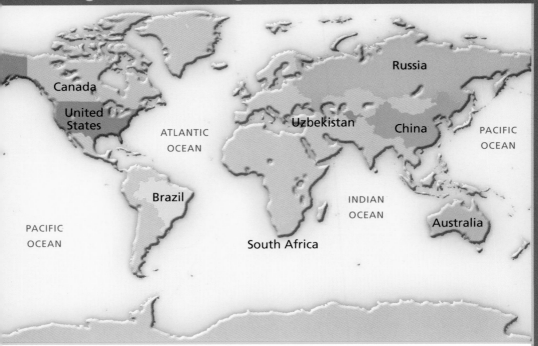

Russia

Canada

United States

Uzbekistan

China

PACIFIC OCEAN

ATLANTIC OCEAN

Brazil

INDIAN OCEAN

Australia

PACIFIC OCEAN

South Africa

Did You Know?

European explorers arrived on the western coast of Africa in 1471. They found so much gold there they called this part of Africa the Gold Coast.

How Gold Is Mined

Mining gold is hard and dangerous work. Underground gold mines are deep below the surface of Earth. Miners enter a steel cage and are lowered into the mine shaft. They use jackhammers and dynamite to blast the ore. Railroad cars bring the ore to the surface.

Then, trucks haul the ore to mills where it is processed. In the mills, the gold is removed from the rock. The gold is melted and poured into molds to make bars of gold. It takes over two million pounds (almost a million kilograms) of ore to make one gold bar.

A lot of land is cleared to build an open-pit mine.

These men are putting explosives into the rock in an underground mine.

A different kind of mining is used to remove ore that is close to the surface. It is called open-pit mining. Bulldozers clear away plants and soil from an area to create an open-pit mine. Miners use explosives and power shovels to dig out the ore. The gold is separated from the ore in the mills.

Did You Know?

The largest gold nugget ever found was in Australia. It produced 142 pounds (64 kilograms) of pure gold!

The Many Uses of Gold

People have used gold since ancient times. For thousands of years, gold has been a symbol of power and riches.

Signs of Power

In ancient Egypt, gold was linked to wealth and power. The Egyptians placed gold at the top of monuments to show that they were powerful. The rulers of ancient Egypt kept much of the gold for themselves. Often, their golden objects were buried with them. One king was buried in a solid gold coffin.

This golden door leads ▶ **to a place where one of the rulers of Egypt was buried.**

Jewelry

Since ancient times, gold has been used to make jewelry. In ancient Egypt, wealthy men and women wore gold jewelry to protect them from evil spirits. Today, gold jewelry is worn for its beauty by people throughout the world. Gold jewelry is made by people called **goldsmiths**. They work with gold to create jewelry and many other objects.

This Indian bride is wearing gold jewelry and clothes made from gold thread to celebrate her wedding. She even has gold dust on her cheeks. ▶

Did You Know?

The word karat is used to tell how much gold is in a piece of jewelry. Pure gold is 24 karats. A 14-karat gold ring is made of 14 parts of gold and 10 parts of other metals.

Money

For thousands of years, gold was used as money. People in the Asian kingdom of Lydia began using gold coins as money in 600 B.C. Countries in Europe began to **mint**, or make, gold coins in 1200 A.D.

Look through the change in your pocket or piggy bank. You won't find any gold coins. The United States has not minted gold coins since the 1930s. At that time, people had to turn in their gold coins. They were given paper money for their gold coins.

The United States stores much of its gold at the Federal Reserve Bank in New York City. It also stores gold at Fort Knox. This building in Kentucky is very safe. It has walls that are over two feet (61 centimeters) thick. It also has many security devices and cameras to protect the gold.

These gold bars are stored in a bank. ▶

Other Uses

Gold conducts, or carries, heat and electricity well. It can be made into wire that is thinner than a strand of hair. Gold wire is used in many electronic devices. It is used in computers, radios, and video cameras. Gold wire connects tiny computer chips to the devices they control.

Gold reflects light. It is used as a shield on space vehicles to keep them from overheating. There is gold on the plastic visors of the helmets astronauts wear. The gold keeps out the harmful rays of the sun. Gold mixed in window glass helps keep offices cool in the summer.

▼ **The shiny gold visor on an astronaut's helmet reflects the sun's rays.**

Gold is even used in medicine. Dentists use gold to repair or replace teeth. Gold is easy to shape and won't dissolve in the mouth.

Gold can be hammered into very thin sheets. The sheets are then used to make **gold leaf**. Gold leaf is used as decoration on books, dishes, glasses, and buildings. Some important buildings have gold domes that are covered with gold leaf.

▲ **This building in Russia has a gold roof.**

Did You Know?

Gold can be hammered into sheets thinner than paper.

The Search for Gold

People have gone on long, dangerous journeys in search of gold. The Spanish explorer, Francisco Vásquez de Coronado, heard stories of a rich empire filled with gold treasures. He decided he wanted to find this golden land called the Seven Golden Cities of Cibola.

In 1540, Coronado left Mexico in search of Cibola. He took with him a large army of Spanish soldiers and Native Americans. They traveled many miles through what is now the southwestern United States.

Coronado led an army in ▶ **search of gold.**

Coronado found Native American villages, but no golden cities. He sent out search parties, but they did not find any gold either.

Coronado returned to Mexico in 1542. He told the government that there were no golden cities. But the story would not die. People continued to search for the Seven Golden Cities of Cibola for many years.

Gold Rushes

When gold was discovered somewhere, people rushed to that place. They all hoped to find gold and get rich.

One famous **gold rush** took place in California. In 1848, a man who was building a sawmill found a few gold nuggets. Word spread that someone had found gold! Soon, thousands of people went there to search for gold.

Prospectors, or people who search for gold, flocked to the area. They claimed land where they thought they would find gold. They panned rivers hoping to find gold nuggets. Some found gold in fields near the surface. Others opened mines. Only a few miners became rich.

▼ **Towns were built in places where gold was found.**

Finding gold became big business. Towns grew up where the miners worked. People invented machines to help get gold out of the mines faster and easier. People opened stores and sold supplies to the miners. These business people had a better chance of getting rich than the miners themselves.

Another gold rush took place in Australia. In 1851, gold was discovered in New South Wales. When people heard this news, they rushed there. Tent cities grew. Overnight, some of these cities had 40,000 people living in them!

▼ **Today, people pan for gold for fun!**

The Search Continues

People are still searching for gold. The rumor of gold draws people to new places. People dream about discovering gold.

People go to museums to look at gold from long ago. They admire the ancient gold jewelry and objects. These gold things have lasted for thousands of years.

Today, gold is still a symbol of success. People who win first prize in contests often receive gold medals. Thousands of years after gold was first discovered, it is still a valuable metal.

Glossary

demand the need or desire for a resource

deposit an underground supply of a resource

empire a large territory controlled by a single person or group

gold a valuable metal

gold leaf thin sheets of gold used to decorate objects or buildings

gold rush a time when many people quickly moved to a place where gold was discovered in hopes of becoming rich

goldsmith a person who works with gold to make objects or jewelry

mint to make money out of a metal

nonrenewable resource a resource that is limited in supply on Earth

ore a rock or mineral that contains a valuable material, such as gold

prospector a person who searches for gold

supply the available amount of a resource

Index